21st Century
Junior
Library

WHAT IS A PLANT?

by Pam Rosenberg

CHERRY LAKE PUBLISHING * ANN ARBOR, MICHIGAN

Published in the United States of America by Cherry Lake Publishing
Ann Arbor, Michigan
www.cherrylakepublishing.com

Content Adviser: Paul Young, MA, Botanist

Reading Consultant: Cecilia Minden-Cupp, PhD, Literacy Specialist and Children's Book Author

Cover and page 4, ©TTphoto, used under license from Shutterstock, Inc.; cover and page 6, ©luchschen, used under license from Shutterstock, Inc.; page 8, ©Beata Becla, used under license from Shutterstock, Inc.; page 10, ©Zacarias Pereira da Mata, used under license from Shutterstock, Inc.; page 12, ©8781118005, used under license from Shutterstock, Inc.; page 14, ©Lepas, used under license from Shutterstock, Inc.; cover and page 16, ©Perov Stanislav, used under license from Shutterstock, Inc.; page 18, ©iStockphoto.com/Bronwyn8; cover and page 20, ©iStockphoto.com/johnnyscriv

LIBRARY OF CONGRESS CATALOGING-IN-PUBLICATION DATA
Rosenberg, Pam.
 What is a plant? / by Pam Rosenberg.
   p. cm.—(21st century junior library)
Includes index.
ISBN-13: 978-1-60279-272-2
ISBN-10: 1-60279-272-0
1. Plants—Juvenile literature. I. Title. II. Series.
QK49.R67 2008
580—dc22   2008012313

Cherry Lake Publishing would like to acknowledge the work of
The Partnership for 21st Century Skills.
Please visit www.21stcenturyskills.org *for more information.*

CONTENTS

There are many different kinds of rosebushes.

Plants Everywhere

Can you give the name of one plant? Maybe your answer would be a rosebush. Or maybe you would say a maple tree. You might even say a cactus.

Cactus plants grow where it is hot and dry.

A rosebush, a maple tree, and a cactus don't look a lot alike. But they are all plants. How can that be? Let's take a look and find out what they have in common.

Look!

Have some fun practicing your looking skills. Grab a notebook and a pencil. Take a walk around your neighborhood. Write down the name or draw a picture of every plant you see. How many different kinds of plants did you find?

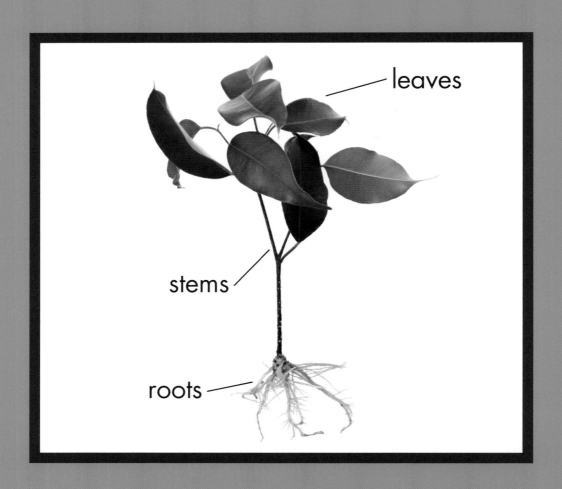

leaves

stems

roots

Can you find the roots, stems,
and leaves on this plant?

Roots, Stems, and Leaves

There are some things that all plants have in common. Plants are living things. They can make their own food. They grow and make new plants. Plants don't move around. Almost all plants have three basic parts: **roots**, **stems**, and **leaves**.

Tree trunks are big, woody stems.

Roots grow down into the ground. They soak up water and **nutrients** that the plant needs to grow. Roots also help keep the plant in the ground.

Stems carry nutrients and water from the roots up to the leaves. They also carry food made by the green leaves to the entire plant. Stems help hold a plant up, too. Some stems are hard and woody. Others are green and can bend.

Leaves come in different sizes and shapes.

Leaves help a plant make food. They collect energy from sunlight. They also have tiny openings. The tiny openings let air and water in and out. A plant uses sunlight, air, and water to make food.

Think!

Plants are just one kind of living thing. Animals are another kind of living thing. Can you think of two ways that plants and animals are the same? How about two ways that they are different?

Some seeds grow inside fruits. Do you see the seeds inside this watermelon?

Growing New Plants

Have you ever seen a **seed**? A bean is a seed you can eat. Can you think of any other kinds of seeds?

Many seeds develop inside flowers. Inside each seed is a tiny plant and some stored food. The tiny plant is called an **embryo**. The stored food helps the embryo begin to grow. The embryo will grow if it has the things it needs.

Plants grow and reach toward the sun.

A plant needs room to grow. Its roots need to spread out. Its stems need to reach up toward the sun. That is because the leaves need sunlight to make food.

Make a Guess!

How many seeds do you think you will find inside one apple? Make a guess. Then ask an adult to help you cut an apple into pieces. Find all of the seeds inside. Count them up. How close was your guess to the number of seeds you found?

Plants need the right amount of water to grow.

A plant needs the right **temperature**. Plants won't grow if it is too cold or too hot. Sunlight, water, and air are needed, too. Remember, plants need all three to make food.

Create!

Drawing pictures can be a good way to remember what you have learned. Pick one kind of plant. Draw a picture of it. Be sure to label its roots, stem, and leaves. Does it have flowers? Draw those, too.

Taking care of a garden will help you learn more about plants.

Grow and Learn

You can learn more about plants by planting your own garden. Pick a spot outside for a garden. Or collect some pots for an indoor garden. Plant some seeds and watch them grow. Make sure they have water, air, and sunlight. Watch carefully and soon you'll be a plant expert!

GLOSSARY

embryo (EM-bree-oh) a tiny plant inside a seed that will develop if the conditions are right

leaves (LEEVZ) the parts of plants that soak up sunlight and make food for the plant

nutrients (NOO-tree-uhnts) things that are needed by plants and animals to grow strong and stay healthy

roots (ROOTS) the parts of plants that grow underground and soak up water and minerals

seed (SEED) the part of a plant that can grow into a new plant

stems (STEMZ) the parts of plants that carry water and minerals to the leaves and carry food made in the leaves to the rest of the plant

temperature (TEM-pur-uh-chur) a measure of how hot or cold it is outside or how hot or cold something is, usually measured with a thermometer

FIND OUT MORE

BOOKS

Hewitt, Sally. *Amazing Plants*. New York: Crabtree Publishing Company, 2007.

Slade, Suzanne. *What Do You Know About Plant Life?* New York: PowerKids Press, 2008.

WEB SITES

Biology4Kids.com: Plants
www.biology4kids.com/files/plants_main.html
Learn more about plants and see pictures of many different kinds of plants

University of Illinois Extension: The Great Plant Escape
www.urbanext.uiuc.edu/gpe/
Read more about plants and find some fun plant activities to try at home

INDEX

ABOUT THE AUTHOR

Pam Rosenberg is a former teacher who currently works as a writer and editor of children's books. She lives in Arlington Heights, Illinois.